HAUNTED! GETTYSBURG

Gareth Stevens
Publishing

BY MICHAEL RAJCZAK

Please visit our website, www.garethstevens.com. For a free color catalog of all our high-quality books, call toll free 1-800-542-2595 or fax 1-877-542-2596.

Library of Congress Cataloging-in-Publication Data

Rajczak, Michael.

Haunted! Gettysburg / by Michael Rajczak.

  p. cm. — (History's most haunted)

Includes index.

ISBN 978-1-4339-9249-0 (pbk.)

ISBN 978-1-4339-9250-6 (6-pack)

ISBN 978-1-4339-9248-3 (library binding)

1. Haunted places—United States—Juvenile literature. 2. Ghosts—United States—Juvenile literature. 3. Ghosts—Pennsylvania—Gettysburg. 4. Haunted places—Pennsylvania—Gettysburg. I. Rajczak, Michael. II. Title.

BF1472.U6 R35 2014

133.1—dc23
First Edition

Published in 2014 by
Gareth Stevens Publishing
111 East 14th Street, Suite 349
New York, NY 10003

Copyright © 2014 Gareth Stevens Publishing

Designer: Nicholas Domiano
Editor: Kristen Rajczak

Photo credits: Cover, p. 1 Jorge Moro/Shutterstock.com; pp. 5, 6 Stringer/Archive Photos/Getty Images; p. 7 UniversalImagesGroup/Universal Image Group/Getty Images; p. 8 Interim Archives/Archive Photos/Getty Images; p. 9 KAREN BLEIER/AFP/Getty Images; p. 10 Buyenlarge/Archive Photos/Getty Images; p. 11 Kean Collection/Archive Photos/Getty Images; p. 13 DeeFabian/Wikimedia Commons; p. 15 Photos.com/Thinkstock; p. 17 Science & Society Picture Library/SSPL/Getty Images; pp. 19, 29 Douglas Graham/CQ-Roll Call Group/Getty Images; p. 21 SAM YU/FREDERICK NEWS-POST/AP Images; p. 23 Stock Montage/Archive Photos/Getty Images; p. 25 Eliot Elisofon/Time & Life Pictures/Getty Images; p. 27 George Eastman House/Archive Photos/Getty Images.

Printed in the United States of America

CPSIA compliance information: Batch #CS13GS: For further information contact Gareth Stevens, New York, New York at 1-800-542-2595.

CONTENTS

Words in the glossary appear in **bold** type the first time they are used in the text.

THE SOLDIERS ON THE TRAIL

One evening, a group of friends were walking along a trail in Gettysburg, Pennsylvania. They had come to take part in a **reenactment** of the famous Battle of Gettysburg. All of a sudden, one stopped and pointed to the side of the trail. A wounded soldier lay there—and they could see through him! Was he a ghost?

Before going back to their hotel, the group met other ghostly soldiers. One was holding a light. Another was marching right toward them. They heard the sounds of other soldiers coming down the path, too. The friends left the trail in terror.

WHAT IS A GHOST?

A ghost is the spirit of a person who has died. Some ghosts take the form of a small misty cloud, streaks, or balls of light that are sometimes seen in photographs. The most commonly reported kind of ghost is one that looks like a person.

The Battle of Gettysburg, shown in this colored print, may have produced many ghosts.

WHAT HAPPENED AT GETTYSBURG?

The Battle of Gettysburg happened during the **American Civil War**. The battle was fought at the beginning of July 1863. The Union army of the North fought the Confederate army from the South in a small town called Gettysburg in Pennsylvania. The fighting was **brutal** and bloody. The Union army won the 3-day battle.

The Battle of Gettysburg was the largest battle that ever took place in the United States. More than 160,000 men fought in it. When it was over, more than 51,000 men had died or were hurt. A national **cemetery** was placed there in memory of the great loss of life.

President Abraham Lincoln spoke at the **dedication** of the Gettysburg cemetery several months after the battle. Now known as the Gettysburg Address, his speech honored those who had fought there. Lincoln said that the country would come out of the war a better nation.

SCATTERED REMAINS

After the battle, bodies of dead soldiers were scattered over 25 square miles (65 sq km). Some were piled together, while other soldiers lay alone. Not all the soldiers' remains were found in time for burial in the new cemetery. Over the years, the remains of more soldiers have been found. In fact, a soldier's skeleton was found in 1996!

7

GHOSTS AT LITTLE ROUND TOP

Some of the spookiest areas of the Gettysburg battlefield are those at which intense fighting happened, such as Little Round Top. The Union army held this hill during the second day of battle. The Confederates launched several attacks but were defeated by a bloody bayonet charge. Many soldiers from both sides died there.

Visitors have reported seeing the ghost of a Union soldier holding his rifle coming from behind the tall rocks of Little Round Top. Men working on a movie about Gettysburg said a ghost here gave them bullets, too. They were the kind that would have been used during the Civil War!

Would you visit Little Round Top at night? You might have to watch out for ghosts!

LED BY A GHOST?

One ghost story of Gettysburg happened during the war. As the Union army approached Gettysburg, it came to a fork in the road. They weren't sure which way to go. Suddenly, a figure on horseback came to the fork and led them toward Little Round Top. The men said this glowing figure was the ghost of George Washington.

9

While making a video of the scenery from Little Round Top, Yvonne Burgamy panned her video camera to the left to include a group of trees. In the distance, there was a bright flash as if a cannon had been fired!

Other people have heard the sounds of gunfire and cannons. Residents of the town of Gettysburg have reported hearing the distant sounds of **bugles**. Still other people have heard drums playing a beat as if soldiers were still marching into battle. These mysterious sights and sounds have been seen and heard at all hours of the day.

Hearing drums and bugles sound from thin air would be eerie. Are soldiers directing battles from beyond the grave?

PLAY THAT TUNE

Bugles and drums were used to send commands and lead troops during battles. Both Union and Confederate armies used such instruments during the Battle of Gettysburg. Buglers played one tune to signal attack and another to signal retreat. Different drumbeats were signals to the soldiers that helped to direct a battle.

11

DEVIL'S DEN

Down the hill from Little Round Top is an area known as Devil's Den. This rocky area has many large boulders, some of which are 20 feet (6 m) high! This provided the perfect place for Confederate **snipers** to hide.

Today, strange things happen at Devil's Den. The batteries in cameras and other electronic devices seem to drain quickly. Images of soldiers and weapons are discovered in pictures taken in Devil's Den. People have reported seeing a barefoot soldier, his uniform no more than rags. On rare occasions, people have seen what appears to be a battle reenactment on days when there is no reenactment there.

WHY DO GHOSTS REMAIN?

Experts claim that when there is a sudden or violent death, a person's spirit may choose to linger where it happened. Some say that these ghosts are confused. Maybe they don't realize they're dead. Perhaps they're afraid to move on. They may feel they still have something they must do.

Hundreds of men died fighting in Devil's Den. One story says a Civil War photographer moved their bodies, which has caused their ghosts to remain—and appear to Gettysburg visitors.

13

One of the most haunted spots at Gettysburg is near Devil's Den. More than 3,000 soldiers died on Triangular Field on the second day of the battle.

Visitors to the field have reported the smells of dead bodies and gunpowder. People who try to use electronic devices such as cameras and video recorders say that even fully charged electronics lose their energy quickly there. In some photographs, the background appears black! The ghosts of Confederate sharpshooters have been seen in the rocks. People have even reported hearing the "rebel yell," a battle cry of the South.

FACING THE HAUNTED

Visiting a place known to be haunted is scary enough. Imagine walking onto Triangular Field and hearing a gunshot and the scream of the soldier who was shot there. Or feeling a sudden spot of cold air as you walk. One visitor had her camera knocked out of her hands by unseen forces.

Would you be brave enough to go to Triangular Field, one of the most haunted places at Gettysburg, at night?

15

FRIGHTENING FIELD HOSPITAL

Pennsylvania Hall of Gettysburg College served as a field hospital during the Battle of Gettysburg. More than a century later, two female staff members were alone in the building while working late one night. They entered an elevator on their way out. Instead of the floor they wanted, the elevator went to the basement.

When the doors opened, the women were shocked by what they saw—wounded and dying soldiers from the Civil War. The smell was awful. One man looked right at them before the doors closed. Panicked, the women told a security guard about what they saw. He said they seemed so scared, he believed their story.

GHASTLY HOSPITALS

Field hospitals during the Civil War weren't like hospitals today. There was very little medicine available. There weren't enough doctors. Soldiers had to suffer through **surgeries**, stitches, and even removal of limbs without painkillers. Soldiers would scream and moan in pain. Many soldiers died from **infection**. It's no wonder their ghosts might haunt an old field hospital.

A field hospital, like the one shown here, was a fearful and bloody place during the Civil War.

17

SACH'S COVERED BRIDGE

In Gettysburg, there's a covered bridge that was used by both the North and the South during the battle. It was one of the routes of retreat for the South as the battle was ending. It's also one of the creepiest places near the battlefield!

Wounded soldiers dying in the Confederate field hospital near the bridge might be one source of restless spirits. It's also said that three men, who may have been spies or **deserters**, were hung from its beams. Visitors report a heavy feeling of sadness when at the bridge. Others report hearing cries, moans, and gunfire there.

GHOSTLY ENERGY

Ghost experts believe that spirits are made of a special kind of energy. When caught in pictures, this energy often appears as small circles of light that you cannot see under ordinary conditions. These balls of light are called orbs. They can sometimes be seen moving through videos recorded in haunted areas.

Some say orbs that show up in photographs are spirits of soldiers who fought at the Battle of Gettysburg.

19

HAUNTED HOUSES IN GETTYSBURG

The Battle of Gettysburg spilled over into the nearby town. Some residents hid in their basements and cellars. Others fled. Area buildings were used as field hospitals and headquarters for military leaders. Many of these buildings still have bullet holes and other scars from the battle. The ghosts of soldiers are said to move in and out of the buildings.

Visitors to Farnsworth House and other historic buildings report being touched by ghostly hands. Strange voices and footsteps are heard. Objects are moved about by the restless spirits who may remain in this haunted town.

THE MOST HAUNTED PLACE IN AMERICA?

How do we know the ghosts left in Gettysburg are from the famous battle? Many ghosts seem to be wearing uniforms of soldiers. Some of these ghostly soldiers appear to be holding their rifles, too. So many people died there during the Civil War, it's no wonder some of their spirits stayed behind.

Gettysburg is a popular place for ghost hunters, or those looking for ghosts, to try to find proof of the **paranormal**. Farnsworth House, which this group is visiting, is one place they often look.

GHOSTLY HORSES OF GETTYSBURG

Did you know that it's possible for animals' ghosts to haunt a place? Around 5,000 horses were killed during the Battle of Gettysburg. Their ghosts are commonly reported.

Visitors have reported hearing the sounds of horses neighing at Sach's Covered Bridge. Some have heard the sound of horses riding across areas of the battlefield. Other people claim that they've felt a cool rush of wind from ghostly horses passing by. Although more rare than the ghosts of people, a few tourists claim that pictures they have taken at the battlefield show the ghosts of horses, some with a soldier riding them.

IMPORTANT BATTLE

The Battle of Gettysburg was one of the bloodiest in American history. However, its importance cannot be overlooked. By losing this battle, the Confederate troops couldn't push the Civil War any farther north. Though the war went on for 2 more years, historians call the Union army's victory the "turning point" of the war.

Troops on horseback are
called cavalry.

23

GHOSTS AT THE CEMETERY

The Soldier's National Cemetery at Gettysburg is the final resting place for over 3,500 Union soldiers. Most of the remains of Confederate soldiers were removed after the war to cemeteries in southern states.

If you visit this peaceful place, you may see a mysterious misty fog hanging close to the ground. People have reported a creepy feeling of being watched. Strange orbs, streaks of light, and cloudy vapors have appeared in photographs taken there. Some people have seen ghostly soldiers walk towards them and then fall to the ground as if they were shot. The ghosts of three Confederate soldiers are said to appear there, too, especially at night.

FINAL RESTING PLACE

Civil War soldiers are no longer the only soldiers buried at Gettysburg. There are graves of soldiers from the Spanish-American War, World Wars I and II, the Korean War, and the Vietnam War. Nearly 1,000 graves belong to Civil War soldiers whose names aren't known.

If visiting a cemetery wasn't creepy enough, imagine walking through one reported to be haunted!

JENNIE WADE

Twenty-year-old Jennie Wade lived in the sleepy town of Gettysburg when Union and Confederate forces arrived. She was the only **civilian** killed during the battle. She was making bread dough on the morning of the third day of battle. A bullet came through two doors of the house and hit Jennie in the back, killing her instantly.

The house she lived in is considered one of the most haunted in the area. Visitors report being touched by ghostly hands. Photographs taken there show strange streaks of light and floating orbs. Some people even claim to have heard Jennie's voice.

EVP

Ghost hunters use sound-recording devices in search of electronic voice **phenomena**, or EVP for short. An EVP is believed to be a spirit talking. Sometimes the voices cannot be heard until a recording is played back. Many ghost hunters ask ghosts questions and claim they receive answers.

JENNIE WADE
LLED JULY 3rd 1863
...BURG PA

Jennie Wade's death was reported in a newspaper—but they spelled her name wrong. Jennie Wade's real name was Ginnie.

GHOST TOURS OF GETTYSBURG

Whether you want to hunt for ghosts or just want to see a historic place, you can visit the town and battlefield of Gettysburg. Visitors can take several different tours of the battlefield and the town. Many of these include spooky stories. Most will take you to the places where ghosts are said to be found.

Perhaps the most interesting tours are called candlelight tours, and they begin around sunset. Imagine the night growing darker and quieter as you head deeper into the lonely battlefield. You could become one of the many people to experience something ghostly!

MARK NESBITT

Some of the most popular ghost tours are based on the work of Gettysburg ghost expert Mark Nesbitt. His interest began when he worked for the National Park Service and heard many stories about this haunted battlefield. He has written several books and appeared on TV shows about the ghosts of Gettysburg and other places.

Would you be brave enough to go on a ghost tour of a haunted battlefield?

GLOSSARY

American Civil War: a war fought from 1861 to 1865 in the United States between the Union (the Northern states) and the Confederacy (the Southern states)

brutal: especially violent or severe

bugle: a kind of horn

cemetery: a place where the dead are buried

civilian: a person not serving in the military

dedication: a ceremony marking the opening of a place

deserter: someone who leaves military service without permission or intention to return

expert: someone with great knowledge about a certain subject

infection: a sickness caused by germs

paranormal: not able to be explained by science

phenomena: extraordinary events

reenactment: repeating events that already happened, often for entertainment

sniper: a soldier specially trained to shoot well from a hiding place

surgery: a medical treatment used for injuries and illnesses that involves operations

FOR MORE INFORMATION

BOOKS

Nesbitt, Mark. *Ghosts of Gettysburg VI: Spirits, Apparitions, and Haunted Places of the Battlefield.* Gettysburg, PA: Second Chance Publications, 2004.

O'Connor, Jim. *What Was the Battle of Gettysburg?* New York, NY: Grosset & Dunlap, 2013.

Shores, Lori. *Ghosts: Truth and Rumors.* Mankato, MN: Capstone Press, 2010.

WEBSITES

American Civil War: The Battle of Gettysburg
www.ducksters.com/history/battle_of_gettysburg.php
Read more about the Battle of Gettysburg and explore links to other information about the important people, places, and events of the American Civil War.

Ghosts of Gettysburg
www.ghostsofgettysburg.com/
Find out more about the candlelight tours of the haunted town and battlefield.

INDEX